ASPCA

PET CARE GUIDES FOR KIDS

RABBIT

Mark Evans

DK

A DK PUBLISHING BOOK

www.dk.com

For Grandma

Project Editor Liza Bruml
Art Editor Jane Coney
Editor Miriam Farbey
Designer Rebecca Johns
U.S. Editor B. Alison Weir
Photographer Steve Shott
Illustrator Malcolm McGregor
ASPCA Consultant Stephen Zawistowski, Ph.D.

First American Edition, 1992
1 3 5 7 9 10 8 6 4 2

Published in the United States by
DK Publishing, Inc., 95 Madison Avenue
New York, New York 10016

Library of Congress Cataloging-in-Publication Data
Evans, Mark.
  Rabbit / Mark Evans. — 1st American ed.
  p. cm. — (ASPCA pet care guides for kids)
  Includes index.
  Summary: Offers information for the first-time pet owner on the
physical characteristics, selection, care, and feeding of rabbits.
  ISBN 0-7894-7653-3
  1. Rabbits—Juvenile literature. [1. Rabbits. 2. Pets.]
I. Title. II. Series.
SF453.2.E82 1992   92-52829
636'.9322—dc20   CIP
                                                    AC
Color reproduction by Colourscan, Singapore
Printed and bound in Spain by Artes Gráficas Toledo, S.A.
D.L. TO: 95 - 2001

Models: Stella Andreou, Jacob Brubert, Martin Cooles,
Minnie Copping, Laura Douglas, Simon Gangadeen,
Steven Gangadeen, Pete Hodson, Corinne Hogarth, Thanh Huynh,
Jason Kerim, Nathalie Lyon, Rachel Mamauag, Paul Mitchell,
Katie Murray, Florence Prowen, Isabel Prowen,
Edward Tillett, Lisa Wardropper

Dorling Kindersley would like to thank everyone who allowed us
to photograph their pet, Jane Burton, Pauline's Pets and Wood Green
Animal Shelters for providing rabbits, Oxford Scientific Films Ltd,
Bridget Hopkinson for editorial help, Christopher Howson for
design help, Salvo Tomasselli for the world map,
and Lynn Bresler for the index.

Picture credits: Paul Bricknell p7 b, p8 tr, p9 b, c, p18 tl, p41 b, p44
tl, b, back cover c; Phillip Dowell p24 tr; Oxford Scientific Films/Eyal
Bartov p13 tr; Tim Shepherd p12 t, p12-13 c

Foreword

Rabbits are really fascinating animals.
They have their own family and are
called lagomorphs, and that sets them
apart and makes them special. They
hop, they wriggle their noses, and they
need your help to be happy and healthy.
What rabbits need, I guess, are you at
your kindest, quietest, most thoughtful,
and responsible best.
Enjoy your rabbit and
please be good and
gentle with it.

Roger Caras
Roger Caras
ASPCA President

Note to parents

This book teaches your child how to be
a caring and responsible pet owner. But
remember, your child must have your
help and guidance in every aspect of
day-to-day pet care. Don't let your child
have a rabbit unless you are sure that
your family has the time and resources
to care for it properly—for the whole
of its life.

Contents

Introduction

The first step to becoming a good rabbit owner is to choose the right kind and size of rabbit, and a suitable hutch. Rabbits with short hair are the easiest to care for. If you get a large rabbit, you must have plenty of space for it to live in. Rabbits like company, but because they can fight with other rabbits, you will make the best friend for your pet. You'll need to care for your rabbit every day. Not just to start with, but for the whole of its life.

Shopping basket full of things you will need

Understanding your pet

You should try to get to know your rabbit well. If you handle it gently and talk to it as often as you can, it will quickly learn to trust you. Watch your pet carefully. You will soon begin to understand the fascinating sounds and other movements it makes to tell you things.

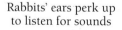

Rabbits' ears perk up to listen for sounds

Caring for your pet

You will be your pet's best friend only if you care for it properly. You will need to make sure that it eats the right foods, always has water, and gets plenty of exercise every day. You will also have to groom it regularly, and keep its hutch clean.

You will need to brush your rabbit every day

Hand feed your rabbit so
it learns to trust you

Things to do with your pet
Your rabbit likes to keep busy. If you play with it every day, you will show everyone that you are a good pet owner.

You will need to visit your
vet's office regularly

People to help
The best rabbit owner always tries to find out more about her pet. The veterinarian at your local vet's office will check that your rabbit is healthy. You can ask anything you like about how to keep your pet fit and happy.

New family member
Your rabbit will be a very special part of your whole family. Everyone will want to pet it, and be interested in what it does. Your rabbit can even become good friends with some of your other pets. You can also introduce it to your friends that like animals.

Your rabbit will
become part of
your family

Ask a grown-up
👭 When you see this sign in the book, you should ask an adult to help you.

Things to remember
When you live with a pet rabbit, there are some important rules you must always follow:

🐾 Wash your hands after petting or playing with your pet, and after cleaning its hutch.

🐾 Don't kiss your rabbit.

🐾 Never give your rabbit food from your plate.

🐾 If your rabbit is hiding or in its bed, don't annoy it.

🐾 Never tease your rabbit.

🐾 Always watch your rabbit when it is with other pets.

🐾 Never, ever hit your rabbit.

What is a rabbit?

Rabbits are members of the leporid family. Leporids have two rows of top front teeth. The sharp front teeth, which never stop growing, are used for gnawing. All leporids belong to a group of animals called mammals. Mammals have warm blood and a hairy body. When they are very young, they drink milk from their mothers.

Life on four legs

Every part of your rabbit does a special job. The hairy coat helps keep your rabbit warm and the oily fur prevents water from soaking down to its skin. Your rabbit has pads of soft, spongy fur under its feet. These protect its toe bones and also give it a good grip when it leaps from place to place.

Long ear is silky

Nose with delicate whiskers

Large back leg

Small front leg

Sharp front teeth

Furry scut

Pink nipple

Belly has soft hair

Underneath your rabbit

Look very closely and you will find that your rabbit has a flat belly button. Count the nipples. Some rabbits have eight. Others have ten. In a mother rabbit, they are sucked for milk by her babies.

Dew claw on front foot

Long hind foot

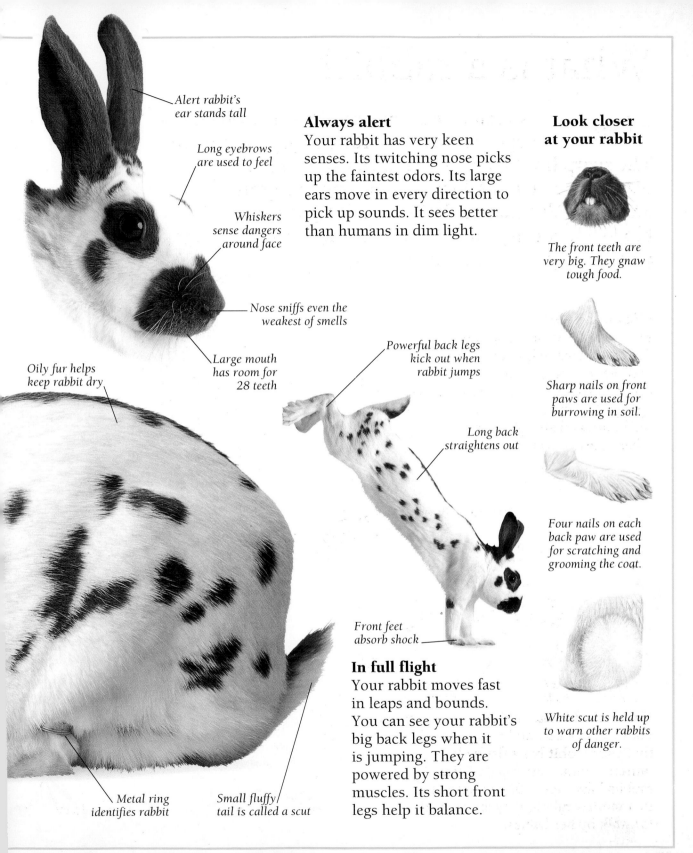

Alert rabbit's ear stands tall

Long eyebrows are used to feel

Whiskers sense dangers around face

Nose sniffs even the weakest of smells

Large mouth has room for 28 teeth

Oily fur helps keep rabbit dry

Metal ring identifies rabbit

Small fluffy tail is called a scut

Always alert
Your rabbit has very keen senses. Its twitching nose picks up the faintest odors. Its large ears move in every direction to pick up sounds. It sees better than humans in dim light.

Powerful back legs kick out when rabbit jumps

Long back straightens out

Front feet absorb shock

In full flight
Your rabbit moves fast in leaps and bounds. You can see your rabbit's big back legs when it is jumping. They are powered by strong muscles. Its short front legs help it balance.

Look closer at your rabbit

The front teeth are very big. They gnaw tough food.

Sharp nails on front paws are used for burrowing in soil.

Four nails on each back paw are used for scratching and grooming the coat.

White scut is held up to warn other rabbits of danger.

Life in the wild

Wild rabbits live together in groups in a warren. A warren has underground rooms, called burrows, which are dug by the females. The burrows are linked by narrow tunnels, and some of them are used only for sleeping. Others, called stops, are lined with fur to make nests for the babies. All the female rabbits in the warren follow a female leader.

Warren door wide enough for one rabbit

Rabbit grazes on grass outside

Long tunnel leads down to nest room

Rabbit stays close to home in case of danger

Wild rabbit has gray, speckled coat

Mother rabbit in the nest she has dug for her young

Nest lined with grass and fur

Life in the warren

Female rabbits make the warren by burrowing. They dig with their front paws, and kick the soil away with their strong back legs. Rabbits sleep in their warren during the day, and graze at dawn and dusk, when their enemies can't see them.

Brave male sits on top of the warren, watching for danger

Young rabbit gnaws at root

Brown hare

Very long ears pick up sounds of danger

Big ears!

Rabbits and hares look very much alike. But hares have bigger ears and their longer legs help them run faster than rabbits. Hares don't dig warrens to live in. Instead they live alone in shallow holes, called forms, that they scrape in the ground.

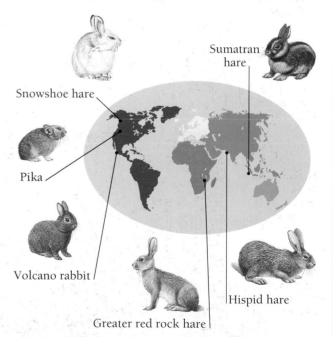

Sumatran hare

Snowshoe hare

Pika

Volcano rabbit

Greater red rock hare

Hispid hare

A worldwide family

Pet rabbits belong to the leporid family. All leporids are members of a group of animals called lagomorphs. The group includes many different kinds of rabbits, hares, and pikas. Lagomorphs live in many parts of the world.

All shapes and sizes

A long time ago, French monks kept wild rabbits for food in walled gardens. They noticed that some rabbits were born with different features—long, shaggy coats or patterned fur. By choosing which rabbits had babies, the monks began to develop different types, or breeds.

Very small, pointed ear

Long ear has black tip

Belgian Hare

Netherland Dwarf

English Lop

Narrow head

Flat nose

Wide head

German Lop

Long and thin nose

Tan

Face shapes
A rabbit's head can be narrow and pointed, or broad and flat. Male rabbits have slightly wider heads than their sisters. The faces of some "lop" breeds of rabbits are so flat that they look as if they have been squashed.

Droopy or perky ears
Most types of rabbits have upright ears, which can be long or short. Sometimes they are nearly as big as a hare's ears. Other types of rabbits have large, floppy ears that touch the ground. They can't hear as well as those rabbits that have upright ears.

Small, medium, large
Wild rabbits are all about the same size. Pet rabbits can be tiny, or very large. The smallest may be called dwarfs or minis. Some huge types are called giants. Find out how big the rabbit that you like the look of will grow.

Medium-sized, slim rabbit

Large ears on "mini" rabbit

Small rabbit has dark ears

Himalayan

Mini-rex

English Lop

Largest breed of rabbit

Flemish Giant

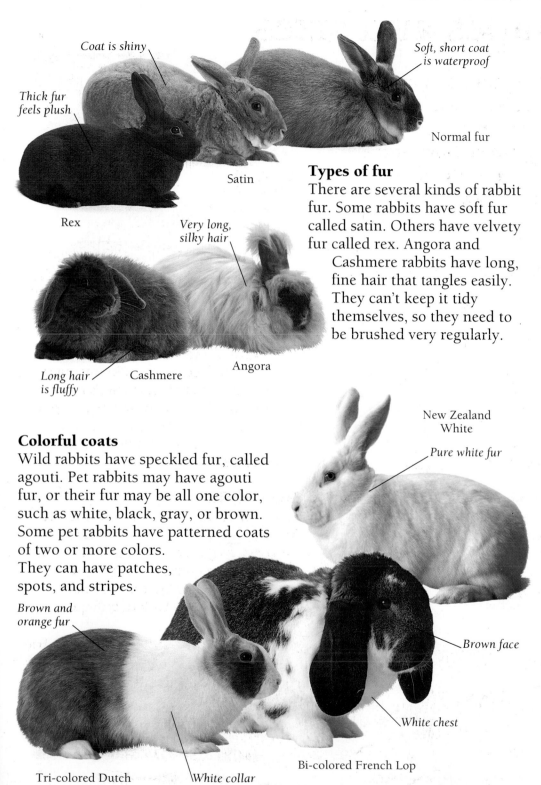

Coat is shiny

Thick fur feels plush

Soft, short coat is waterproof

Normal fur

Satin

Rex

Types of fur
There are several kinds of rabbit fur. Some rabbits have soft fur called satin. Others have velvety fur called rex. Angora and Cashmere rabbits have long, fine hair that tangles easily. They can't keep it tidy themselves, so they need to be brushed very regularly.

Very long, silky hair

Long hair is fluffy Cashmere

Angora

Colorful coats
Wild rabbits have speckled fur, called agouti. Pet rabbits may have agouti fur, or their fur may be all one color, such as white, black, gray, or brown. Some pet rabbits have patterned coats of two or more colors. They can have patches, spots, and stripes.

Brown and orange fur

New Zealand White

Pure white fur

Brown face

White chest

Tri-colored Dutch _White collar_

Bi-colored French Lop

How a rabbit gets its looks

Two rabbits of the same breed have an identical baby.

The baby looks the same as its parents.

Two different breeds of rabbit will produce a mix, or crossbred.

The baby looks a little like each of its parents.

The baby of two crossbred rabbits can look like almost anything.

The offspring is a real mixture.

15

Your rabbit's home

Before you go to pick up your rabbit, you must get it a hutch to live in. Rabbits are very active, so the hutch must have plenty of space. Put the hutch in a sheltered place, where it is safe from any other animals. Remember to stock up with rabbit food (see p. 24). You will also need to buy bedding, litter, and feeding equipment.

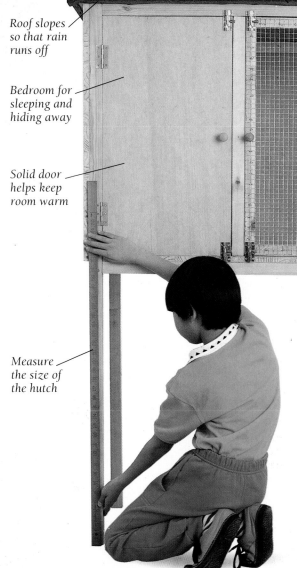

Roof overhangs to protect from rain

Roof slopes so that rain runs off

Bedroom for sleeping and hiding away

Solid door helps keep room warm

Measure the size of the hutch

Sheets of paper
You need some large pieces of paper to line the floor of the hutch. Old drawing paper or newspaper is ideal.

Wood shavings

Hay

Straw

Lining the hutch
Buy wood shavings to put on the hutch floor. These soak up urine. Buy straw for your rabbit to make its bed in. Get some fresh, dry hay for your rabbit to eat.

Hay rack
Buy a hay rack to fix to the hutch door. Your rabbit can pull hay from it to eat. The hay will be kept clean in the rack because your pet cannot trample it.

Apple tree branch

Gnawing log
Find a small tree branch for your rabbit to gnaw on. Gnawing helps keep the teeth healthy. A branch from an untreated fruit tree is best.

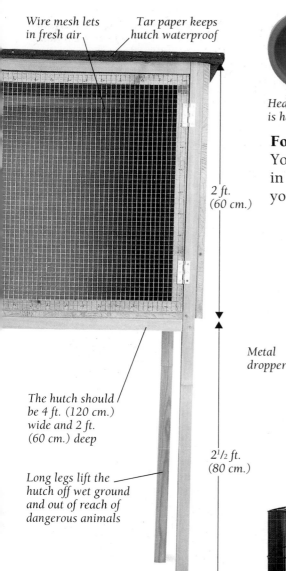

Wire mesh lets
in fresh air

Tar paper keeps
hutch waterproof

2 ft.
(60 cm.)

The hutch should
be 4 ft. (120 cm.)
wide and 2 ft.
(60 cm.) deep

Long legs lift the
hutch off wet ground
and out of reach of
dangerous animals

2½ ft.
(80 cm.)

The hutch
👫 Look at the measurements in the picture. This hutch is just large enough for a small rabbit. If you get two rabbits or a large rabbit, the hutch should be bigger. All hutches must have two rooms. The large room is a living room, the small room is a bedroom.

Bowl
Buy a large food bowl. It must not be plastic because your rabbit may gnaw it.

Heavy bowl
is hard to tip

Food container
You need a container in which to store your rabbit's food.

Airtight box
keeps food fresh

Metal
dropper

Water bottle
Buy a water bottle with a dropper. The dropper lets out water when your rabbit sucks the end of the metal tube.

Mineral lick
Rabbits need to eat plenty of mineral salts. Buy a special salt lick.

Indoor cage
You can also keep your rabbit indoors. It needs a small cage to sleep in. The cage must be big enough for your rabbit to stretch out in when it is lying on its side.

Where to put the hutch

Make sure cats and
other animals can't
get into the hutch.

Keep the rabbit
hutch shaded from
bright sunshine.

Shelter the rabbit
hutch from wind
and rain.

Bitter cold
weather will
freeze your rabbit.

Put the hutch in a
place where you can
look at it often.

17

Getting ready

You will need to get some special equipment for taking care of your new pet. It does not need to be expensive, but it should be well made, because rabbits chew everything they find. Make sure the equipment is ready before you bring your rabbit home.

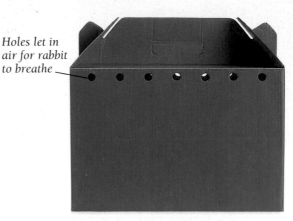

Holes let in air for rabbit to breathe

Cardboard carrying box
Ask your vet for a special box in which to carry your rabbit.

Old tray

Sliding pin keeps lid firmly closed

Wire basket
You can get a strong wire cage to carry your rabbit in. It will last longer than the carrying box.

Weighing scale
You will need to weigh your rabbit to check that it is healthy. Find an old kitchen scale to weigh a young or small rabbit. Weigh a larger rabbit on a bathroom scale.

Rounded prongs won't scratch your rabbit

Grooming equipment
Your rabbit's hair will become tangled. Buy a small, soft brush and a fine comb to keep it clean and neat.

Brush   Comb

Tightly fitting lid keeps litter fresh

Plastic garbage bin

Scoop

Litter tray liners

Indoor rabbit equipment
If you keep your rabbit indoors, it will go to the bathroom in a litter tray. Buy a storage bin for the litter, plastic tray liners, and a scoop to fill and empty the tray.

Litter tray

Clay

Straw

Wood chips

Garden dirt

Litter tray and litter

A cat litter tray is just the right size for an indoor rabbit to use. Try different kinds of litter to see which your rabbit prefers.

Grazing ark

Buy or make a grazing ark so that your rabbit can run around and graze outside. The ark must have a covered area so your rabbit can shelter from the sun or hide if it is scared.

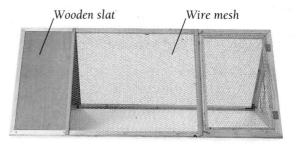

Wooden slat   *Wire mesh*

Detergent   Disinfectant   Bucket   Scrubbing brush   Dustpan   Dustpan brush

Scraper   Rubber gloves   Bottle brush   Spout brush

Cleaning equipment

To clean your rabbit's hutch, you will need some special equipment. Never take items that are used to clean your house. Ask your veterinarian what type of disinfectant spray to buy. Keep all the cleaning equipment together, so it is not used to clean anything else.

Choosing your rabbit

You can choose a baby rabbit from a litter when it is six weeks old. The babies look so cuddly that you may want to take them all home. Only get more than one rabbit if you have a very big hutch (see p. 17). If you have room for two, select baby females, because two males may fight.

Young kitten   Full-grown adult

Big or small?
Find out how big the type of rabbit you want will grow. Some types of rabbits can become very large and need to live in a big hutch.

Baby or adult?
It is easy to fall in love with a tiny baby rabbit, called a kitten. But remember, a kitten will soon grow up. An adult rabbit will be just as adorable.

Where to buy your rabbit
- A friend's rabbit may have babies.
- A breeder will have breed rabbits.
- An animal shelter may have all kinds of rabbits that need homes.

1 **When you go to choose** a baby rabbit, watch the litter with the owner from outside the enclosure. Try to spot the most playful kitten.

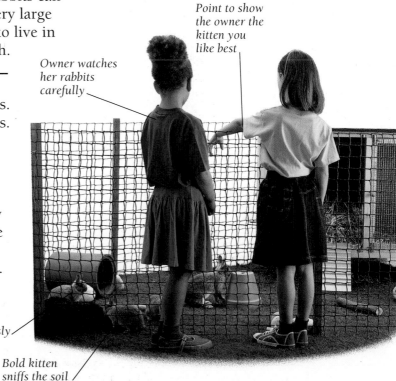

Point to show the owner the kitten you like best

Owner watches her rabbits carefully

Kitten looks around curiously

Bold kitten sniffs the soil

2 Ask the owner to pick up the kitten that you think is the liveliest. Ask whether it is a male or a female. Remember, if you want to keep two rabbits, choose females. Check that the kitten hasn't already been chosen by anyone else.

Hungry mother nibbles at carrot

Owner sits to hold your favorite kitten

3 The owner will let you hold the kitten. Make sure you are sitting down. Put the kitten on your lap so it feels safe. It should be very friendly. Now you can decide if you really like it.

Mother rabbit listens for threatening noises

Gently stroke the kitten's ears

One hand keeps the kitten steady

Cradle rabbit on its back to check the fur on its belly

Carrying box to put your rabbit in on the trip home

4 Check that the rabbit is healthy. Ask the owner to show you how to pick it up. The rabbit should have bright eyes, and a clean nose and ears. The fur should be soft and dry all over. Remember to check the hidden places, like under the scut.

Stay sitting down to do the health checks

Welcome home

Your new rabbit may be frightened when it first leaves its mother. You must have the hutch ready so that your new pet will settle down quickly. Cover the floor with paper and shavings. Put lots of straw in the bedroom and some in the living room. Fill the hay rack, food bowls, and water bottle. Don't forget a gnawing log.

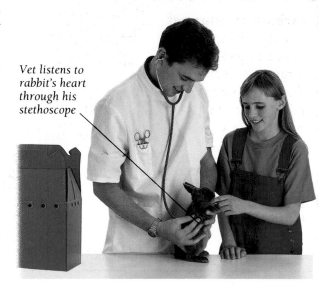

Vet listens to rabbit's heart through his stethoscope

Visiting your veterinarian

Arrange to visit your vet on the way home from picking up your new rabbit. He will examine it all over to make sure that it is healthy. Your vet will answer any questions you have about your new pet.

Vet looks to determine the sex

Checking the sex

When a rabbit is very young, it can be hard to tell if it is a male or a female. Ask your vet to check the sex of your rabbit, so you are sure it is the sex you wanted.

Male rabbit

Female rabbit

Males and females

The two pictures will help you find out the sex of your pet. Look between its back legs.

Attach water bottle to door

Fix salt lick to wire mesh door

Spread wood shavings on the floor

Picking up your pet

Small rabbits are easier to pick up than large ones (see p. 31). To pick up a small rabbit, put one hand over its neck, and the other hand under its bottom. Scoop it up.

Be careful not to pull the ears

Hold your rabbit close to your chest

When to handle your new rabbit

Day 1: Put your rabbit in its hutch. Watch it, but don't disturb it.

Day 2: Your rabbit may hide in its bed. Talk to it, so it gets used to your voice.

Days 3 to 5: Offer your rabbit food from your hand. Pet it, and try to pick it up.

Days 6 to 14: Pet and brush your rabbit. Introduce it to your other pets (see p. 35).

After 2 weeks: Play with your rabbit every day. Let your rabbit out in its enclosure and grazing ark.

Your rabbit's new home

Carefully lift your rabbit out of its carrying box and into its hutch. Lock the doors, and leave it to explore its new home. Come back often to check that it is settling down.

Fill hay rack with fresh hay

Put some straw in the living room

Bolt the door to keep it firmly closed

Feeding your rabbit

Rabbits are herbivores, which means they eat only plants. In the wild, they graze on seeds, roots, and wild grasses. To keep your rabbit fit, you must feed it the same kind of food. You should give it specially prepared rabbit food. You can also take your rabbit out of its hutch to graze on grass (see p. 38).

Razor-sharp teeth bite off portions of food

Side teeth grind food

Mouth made for chewing
The food your rabbit eats needs to be well chewed. A rabbit's teeth and mouth are specially made for grinding and biting. Food is mixed with saliva in the mouth while it is ground by the teeth.

Grazing all day
Grass and some wild plants are favorite foods for rabbits. They have to eat a lot of greens to get enough nutrients. Given the chance, your rabbit will spend many hours nibbling every day.

Dried food

Special foods
Even if your rabbit grazes on grass, you need to give it other food. It loves hay, which is dried grass. You must also buy your rabbit special food made from mixtures of dried plants, seeds, and vegetables.

Hay is kept clean and tidy in the rack

Hay

Your rabbit spends a lot of time eating

When to feed your rabbit
Feed your rabbit every morning and evening. It must always have dried food to eat. Your rabbit won't make a store of food, like a squirrel or a hamster will.

Eating droppings

🐾Do not worry if you see your rabbit eating its own droppings—all rabbits do this. Your rabbit's stomach can't take all the nutrients from food the first time it eats it. So your pet makes soft droppings, which it eats again. Its next droppings will be small, round, and hard.

Tip of tube has a little ball in it to stop water from dripping

Fresh water

Wild rabbits get water from the fresh food they eat. Your rabbit eats a lot of dried food, so you must make sure that its water bottle is always full.

Screw lid on tightly

Fresh water

Pour fresh food into the bowl every morning and evening

An apple tree log is best

Grinding down teeth

Your rabbit's teeth grow all the time. Wild rabbits eat hard food, which wears down their teeth. Give your rabbit a log to gnaw. This will stop its teeth from growing too long.

How much to feed your rabbit

Each time you feed your rabbit, fill its bowl to the brim. Your rabbit should only eat as much food as it needs. If it has plenty of exercise, it won't get fat.

Feeding fresh foods

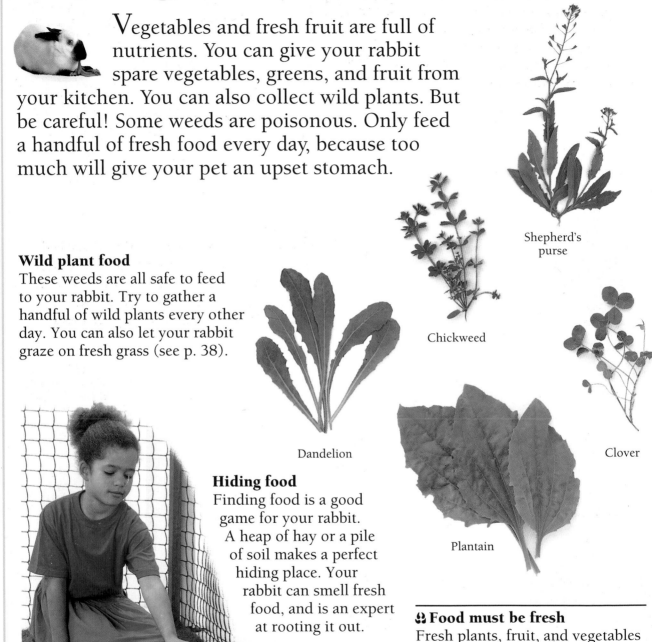

Vegetables and fresh fruit are full of nutrients. You can give your rabbit spare vegetables, greens, and fruit from your kitchen. You can also collect wild plants. But be careful! Some weeds are poisonous. Only feed a handful of fresh food every day, because too much will give your pet an upset stomach.

Wild plant food

These weeds are all safe to feed to your rabbit. Try to gather a handful of wild plants every other day. You can also let your rabbit graze on fresh grass (see p. 38).

Shepherd's purse

Chickweed

Dandelion

Clover

Plantain

Hiding food

Finding food is a good game for your rabbit. A heap of hay or a pile of soil makes a perfect hiding place. Your rabbit can smell fresh food, and is an expert at rooting it out.

Heap of soil for digging in

🐾 Food must be fresh

Fresh plants, fruit, and vegetables quickly become stale. Throw away these foods if they haven't been eaten by bedtime. Never give your rabbit grass cuttings because they turn moldy very quickly.

Favorite fruits

🧑🧑 Feed some fresh fruit to your rabbit every day. Give it half an apple, a whole tomato, or a small slice of melon. Wash the fruit before giving it to your rabbit to nibble.

Green tomatoes

Apple

Tomatoes

Pear

Melon

Kale

Celery

Snow peas

Vegetable treats

🧑🧑 Every day, chop up a handful of washed vegetables to give to your rabbit. Try to find leftovers in your kitchen. You could also ask your greengrocer for some scraps that are suitable. Always make sure they are fresh.

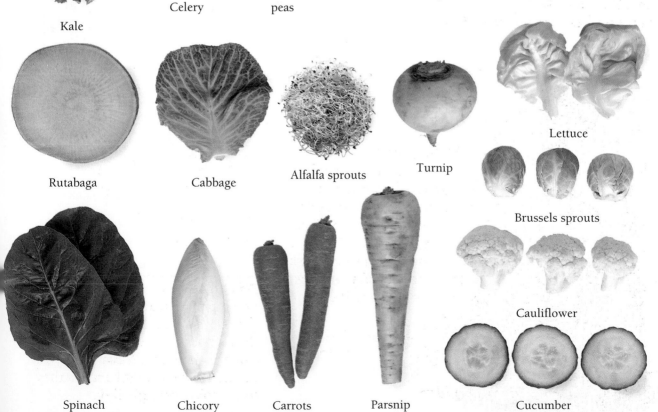

Rutabaga

Cabbage

Alfalfa sprouts

Turnip

Lettuce

Brussels sprouts

Cauliflower

Spinach

Chicory

Carrots

Parsnip

Cucumber

Cleaning the hutch

Your rabbit likes its home to be very clean. If the hutch becomes dirty, it will start to smell and your rabbit may become ill. You should clean out the hutch and wash the feeding equipment every day. When you have finished, put down new paper and fresh straw, shavings, and hay. Make sure the food bowl, hay rack, and water bottle are full. Once a week, scrub out the hutch thoroughly.

1 **Every day, put your rabbit** in its carrying box. This will keep it safely out of the way while you clean the hutch. On a dry day, let your rabbit outside in its enclosure or grazing ark. Don't forget to take the rack, bowl, and water bottle out of the hutch for cleaning.

Remember to pull up all the paper

Reach to sweep the very back of the hutch

2 **Use your dustpan and brush** to sweep up the old straw, wood shavings, droppings, and stale food. Wear the rubber gloves to keep your hands clean. Lift up all the lining paper. Throw away everything into a garbage bin.

Don't scrape too hard, or you will damage the wood

3 Use your scraper to lift off any bits that are stuck to the floor or sides of the hutch. The corners will be dirtiest. Sweep up with the dustpan and brush.

Spray to kill germs   *Scrub hard*

Bucket of hot, soapy water

Thorough cleaning

Once a week, use a brush and hot, soapy water to scrub the inside of the hutch. Rinse the hutch and then spray it with disinfectant. Allow it to dry completely.

Washing the bowl

Wipe out the food bowl with the cloth. Soak it first if it is dirty. Dry it with a paper towel.

Wipe the cleaning cloth all around the bowl

Emptying the rack

Remove any uneaten hay from the hay rack. Don't throw the hay away. You can use it as bedding. Pack the rack with fresh hay for your rabbit to eat.

Clear drinking tube

Make sure nothing is blocking the bottle dropper. Brush the tube with the spout brush. Then shake the tube. You should hear the ball move.

Twist the brush inside the tube

Turn the brush to clean the sides

Clean water bottle

Pour hot, soapy water into the bottle. Scrub inside with the bottle brush. Rinse the bottle before filling it with cold, fresh water.

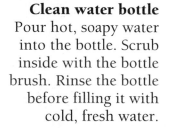

Grooming your rabbit

Your rabbit gets dirt and straw stuck in its coat. In spring, thick winter fur starts to loosen and fall out. This is called molting. To keep itself clean, your rabbit grooms itself. You can help your pet stay neat by brushing it every day. Brushing also helps it get used to being handled. If you have a Cashmere or an Angora, grooming untangles the long hair.

Paws are covered in saliva, like soap, to clean face

Licked clean
A rabbit spends a lot of time grooming itself. It uses its front teeth as a comb to pick out dirt, and its tongue as a washcloth. It wipes its face with its front paws.

Don't forget the fur on the tips of the Angora's ears

Brush one section of the fur at a time

Brushing short hair
To groom a short-haired rabbit, brush the hair on its back away from its head. Next brush its belly, and under its chin. Then comb all the parts in the same order.

Rosette for the owner of prize-winning rabbit

Brush the back from the head to the tail

Best groomed rabbit wins prize

Grooming long hair
The hair of a Cashmere or Angora gets so tangled that it must be groomed a little bit at a time. Choose a part of the coat. Brush the hair, then comb it, then brush it again. Then choose another part.

Picking up a large rabbit

Kneel down next to your pet

1 **Before picking up a** large rabbit, spread out a towel on the floor next to your pet. Sit down beside the towel. Gently nudge your rabbit onto the towel.

Pet and cuddle your rabbit, so that it feels very safe

Lay large towel flat on floor

Rabbit sits facing your knees

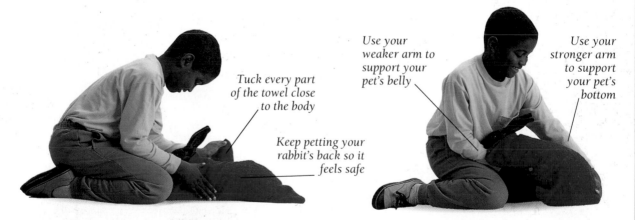

Tuck every part of the towel close to the body

Keep petting your rabbit's back so it feels safe

Use your weaker arm to support your pet's belly

Use your stronger arm to support your pet's bottom

2 **Fold both sides of the towel** over your rabbit's back. Make sure every part of its body is covered except for its face and ears. Your rabbit will feel secure when it is wrapped up. It will not be able to wriggle when you pick it up.

3 **Lift your rabbit off the floor.** Put one hand under its bottom and the other under its belly. When you have scooped up your pet, hold it close to your chest. Stand up only when you are sure that your rabbit is comfortable.

Understanding your rabbit

Your rabbit makes soft grunts, but these won't tell you its mood. Your rabbit will squeal when it is frightened. It also warns other rabbits of danger by thumping its back legs. A rabbit finds out a lot by sniffing. It can even tell from another rabbit's smell whether it is a friend or enemy. Watch your rabbit, and you will soon understand much of what it is doing.

Eye is nearly closed

Cuddling together
Rabbit kittens are very friendly. The brothers and sisters huddle together in a heap when they are sleeping. This helps keep them warm.

Rabbit nuzzles its friend's chin

Marking what's mine
Your rabbit rubs a special scent, which is made in its skin, onto everything in its hutch, grazing ark, and enclosure. If your rabbit lives with another rabbit, it rubs its friend's chin to leave the scent.

Ears perk up to listen

Eyes search for danger

Best of friends
Your rabbit will show you that you are its friend. It rubs its head against you to leave its special scent. It may even wash you with its tongue!

Keeping a lookout
When your rabbit hears a strange sound, it stands up on its hind legs to see what is happening.

Friendly rabbit licks your fingers

Standing up allows rabbit to see farther

Rabbit sits happily on your lap

Signaling danger

When a mother rabbit thinks that her kittens are in danger, she will stand in front of them. If she is very worried, she will thump the ground with her back leg. This tells the kittens, and other nearby rabbits, to run for cover.

Mother rabbit shelters babies behind her

Back leg slams onto the ground

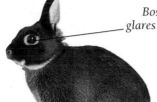

Timid rabbit twists head away in fear

Bossy rabbit glares at enemy

Meeting the enemy

A rabbit may become angry with another rabbit. It will stare straight at its enemy to let the other know that it is annoyed.

Show of strength

If the timid rabbit doesn't run away, both rabbits will scratch the ground with their front paws. They may run at each other.

Claws scrape the ground

Head turns to avoid bite

Teeth grab enemy's neck

Back leg may kick out

The fight

If neither rabbit is scared away, a fight begins. They charge forward and try to sink their teeth into each other's necks.

The loser

The weaker rabbit runs away when it is beaten. It will never forget the other rabbit's scent. Whenever it smells the other rabbit's scent, it will avoid it.

Friends for your pet

Your rabbit will get very lonely without any friends. In the wild, rabbits live in groups in a large warren. When two rabbits are kept together in a small hutch, they may fight. Unless you have a hutch that is large enough for two rabbits, you make the best friend for your pet.

Sisters are best!
You can keep two rabbits together if they are females. Two sisters from the same litter will get along best. You must have a very big hutch and a large enclosure.

Male rabbit does not help care for babies

The rabbit family
Do not keep a male and a female rabbit together unless you want them to have babies. Male and female rabbits kept in the same hutch will fight most of the time.

Babies suck milk from their mother's nipples

A rabbit each
If your brother or sister gets a rabbit, keep it in a separate hutch, unless both rabbits are baby females. Spend a lot of time with your pet to keep it from being lonely.

You can be your rabbit's best friend

Pet fur along back toward tail

Be ready to pick your rabbit up if it is frightened

Your rabbit sits happily while you pet it

Rabbit sniffs the dog curiously

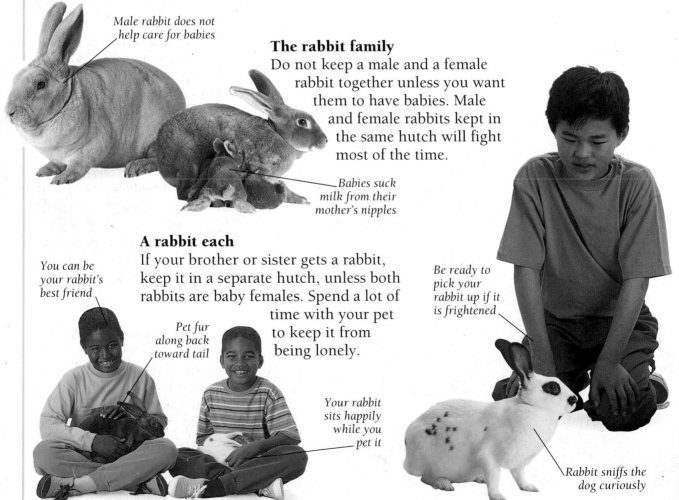

Rabbit sits very still

Bird friend
A small pet bird, such as a budgerigar, can make good friends with your rabbit. Your rabbit knows that the tiny bird is too small to harm it.

Meeting a dog
You can introduce your rabbit to a well-behaved dog, but never leave them alone together. Do not let your cat and rabbit meet. Your cat may attack your rabbit and frighten it.

Gently pet the dog to keep him calm

Always hold the leash firmly

Leaving your pet

Going on vacation
You can't always take your rabbit with you when you go on vacation. You must find someone to take care of it. You may have a friend with a rabbit who has time to look after yours as well.

Making a checklist
Make a list of the jobs that need doing every day, in the order that you do them. Your rabbit is used to this order and may be upset if it is changed. Note the name and telephone number of your vet.

What to pack
Get everything ready for your friend. Make sure you pack enough food, bedding, and litter to last until you get back. Don't forget all the cleaning and grooming equipment.

Moving your rabbit
Take your rabbit to your friend in its carrying box, wire basket, or small, indoor cage. Bring your grazing ark with you if your friend has nowhere for your pet to exercise.

The indoor rabbit

You can keep your rabbit indoors if you don't have a yard. Your rabbit will need a special cage to sleep in and a litter tray in which to go to the bathroom. Your rabbit should spend most of the day out of its cage. Only keep two rabbits indoors if they are friends (see p. 34). They must have separate cages. If you have other pets, beware—they may not want to be friends with your rabbit.

Litter-training your pet
You must train your rabbit to go to the bathroom in its litter tray, or it will make a mess. Put it in the tray every few minutes. Your rabbit will soon learn to go to the tray by itself.

Cover the bottom of the tray with litter

Plastic liner

Naughty rabbit!
👭 Your rabbit may try to chew and scratch the things in your home. If you see your rabbit being naughty, say "No" in a loud voice. If your pet doesn't stop, spray it with some water.

Point firmly at your rabbit

Rabbit tries to chew leaves

Rabbit sniffs sofa curiously

Small cage for one rabbit to sleep in

The indoor cage

Your rabbit will sleep overnight in a cage. Get the biggest cage that you can. Cover the base with a layer of paper, wood shavings, and straw. Put the cage in a safe corner, away from other pets. You must empty and clean it every day.

Carefully put your rabbit into its cage

Attach a water bottle filled with fresh water

Hay for your rabbit to eat

Make sure wires are out of reach of your rabbit

Dangers in the home

Keep electric cords out of reach of your pet.

Sharp objects may cut your pet.

Some dogs may harm your rabbit (see p. 35).

Hot drinks may spill and burn your rabbit.

Keep doors closed so your pet can't escape.

Be careful that no one steps on your pet.

Keeping busy

Your rabbit is very active. Playing around your house helps keep it fit. You should let it out of the cage as much as possible. Always watch your rabbit to make sure that it is safe and does not damage anything in your house.

Litter tray filled with litter

Large bowl of water

Dried food in bowl

Paper keeps floor clean

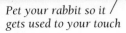

Pet your rabbit so it gets used to your touch

Rabbit looks for the next place to explore

The outdoor rabbit

Your rabbit loves to be outside. Ask an adult to help you make a corner of your backyard into an enclosure. Make sure the wire fencing is buried into the ground or your rabbit may be able to burrow its way out of the enclosure. Stand the hutch in one corner, and put things in the area for your rabbit to play with. You should let your rabbit out of its hutch every day to exercise and graze.

Eating fresh grass
You can use the lid from an indoor rabbit's cage as a small grazing ark. Your rabbit will quickly nibble the patch of grass, so move the lid often. Always watch your rabbit when it is outside.

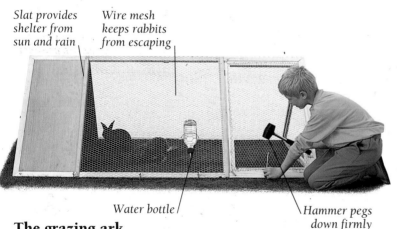

Slat provides shelter from sun and rain

Wire mesh keeps rabbits from escaping

Water bottle

Hammer pegs down firmly

The grazing ark
Your rabbit likes to eat fresh grass every day. You can make or buy a grazing ark. Every day, put your rabbit on the grass in the ark. Remember to peg the ark down so your rabbit can't tip it up, and other animals can't get inside. Move the ark each day so your rabbit always has fresh grass to nibble.

Heap of soil

Rocks are good for exploring

Hide food in flower pot

The rabbit enclosure

It is fun to watch your rabbit play in its enclosure. If you have two rabbits, they may each need a hutch inside the enclosure (see p. 17). When you are not watching your rabbit, cover the area with wire mesh to stop other animals from getting in.

(see p. 17)

Beware of outdoor dangers

Prowling cats may jump into the area.

Birds of prey may swoop down.

Weedkillers on grass are poisonous.

Dogs may scare your rabbit.

Some plants will poison your pet.

Shelter the area from bad weather and bright sun.

Wire fence surrounds enclosure

Wire mesh lets fresh air in and keeps danger out

Plastic sheet to cover area when it rains

Ramp for rabbits to climb down

Fresh grass to nibble

Feed your rabbit by hand

Having babies

Just as a grown-up woman may have children, a female rabbit can have baby rabbits, called kittens. You must think very carefully before keeping female and male rabbits together to breed. You will have to find good homes for all of the kittens. There may be as many as eight in a litter. Your vet may be able to give your rabbit a neutering operation. This stops it from having babies.

✿Responsible owner

It may seem like fun to let your female rabbit have kittens. But don't forget that these cuddly balls of fluff soon grow up. You will need to find each of them a new home.

Eye closed

Fur has begun to grow

Four-day-old kitten

1 **When a kitten is born** it can't see or hear. It has a keen sense of smell, so it can find its mother for a drink of milk. After four days, its fur starts to grow.

2 **Two-week-old kittens drink milk** from their mother. The milk gives them all the nutrients they need to grow. The mother usually only lets the kittens drink once a day for about five minutes. Then she leaves them alone in the nest she has built for them.

Eye open so kitten can see

Kitten hears through long ear

Mother keeps a lookout

Kitten burrows in for a drink

3 **At five weeks old**, the kittens have left their mother. They can eat solid food. They play with their brothers and sisters. When they are tired, they huddle together to keep warm. They will soon be ready to go to new homes.

Playful kitten tries to climb on top

Kitten cuddles up to keep warm

Kitten sniffs for scents

4 **When a rabbit is five months old**, it looks like a small grown-up. Both male and female rabbits are now ready to have a family of their own. Keep them apart, unless you want your rabbits to breed.

Fur is thick and sleek

5 **As a rabbit grows older**, its body grows plumper and its back legs grow stronger. It needs to have a friend. You can become its best friend. You can also keep it with another rabbit in a very large hutch (see p. 17).

Pet your rabbit to show that you are its friend

Powerful back leg

Health care

You need to care for your rabbit properly to make sure it stays healthy. You should give it the right food (see p. 24), keep it well groomed (p. 30), and make sure that it has plenty of room to exercise. You also need to do some simple health checks with your rabbit every day. You will learn to tell quickly if your pet is unwell. If you think something is wrong, take it to your veterinarian.

Push the fur backward

1 **Check that your rabbit's coat** is in good condition. You can do this when you groom your pet. Push the fur backward so you can see down to the skin. The fur should feel soft and smell clean. Don't forget to look at its belly and under the scut.

Carefully pull back the ear-flap

2 **Examine your rabbit's ears.** Hold the ear very gently between your fingers. Look down the dark hole. The ear should be clean. If it smells, your rabbit might be ill.

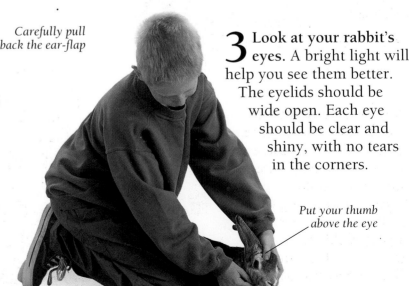

3 **Look at your rabbit's eyes.** A bright light will help you see them better. The eyelids should be wide open. Each eye should be clear and shiny, with no tears in the corners.

Put your thumb above the eye

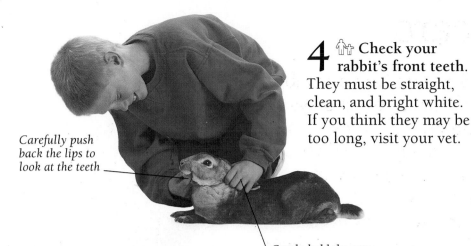

Carefully push back the lips to look at the teeth

4 👫 **Check your rabbit's front teeth.** They must be straight, clean, and bright white. If you think they may be too long, visit your vet.

Gently hold the ears flat against the back to stop your rabbit from wriggling

Toenail is too long

Toenail is right length

5 **Pick up and check each paw in turn.** Look carefully between the toes and underneath at the furry pads. Make sure nothing is stuck in the hair. Don't forget to check that the toenails are the right length.

Grip the paw between your thumb and fingers

Weighing your rabbit
Weigh your rabbit at the same time, on the same day, every week. Write down the weight. Wash the weighing tray thoroughly afterward. If your rabbit has lost or gained weight, it may be ill, or it may not be getting enough exercise.

Line the tray with paper

Old scale

Visiting your veterinarian

The veterinarians and the veterinary assistants who work at your local vet's office want to help you keep your rabbit happy and healthy. They will tell you how to care for your rabbit properly. You can ask them as many questions as you like. They will also try to help make your rabbit better if it gets ill.

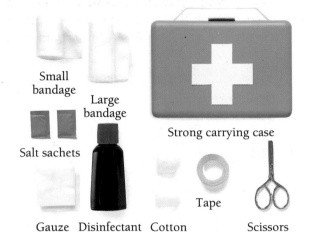

Small bandage

Large bandage

Strong carrying case

Salt sachets

Tape

Gauze pads

Disinfectant

Cotton balls

Scissors

The first aid kit
Prepare a special first aid kit for your rabbit. The veterinary assistant will explain to you how to use everything. Just like you, your pet may scrape or cut itself by accident. The kit contains all the things you will need to make it feel better on the way to the vet's office.

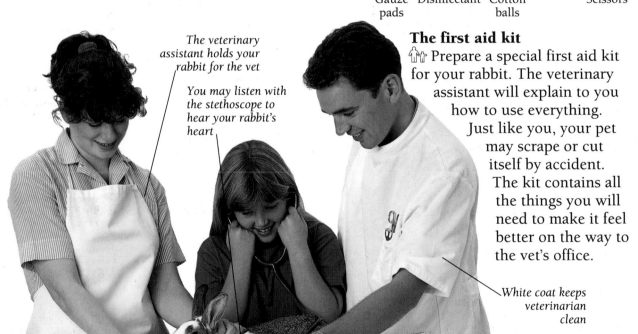

The veterinary assistant holds your rabbit for the vet

You may listen with the stethoscope to hear your rabbit's heart

White coat keeps veterinarian clean

Your veterinary assistant
The veterinary assistant helps the vet. She knows a lot about rabbits. If you have any questions about your pet, visit or call the veterinary assistant at your vet's office.

Your veterinarian
The veterinarian will give your pet special health checks. If your pet is ill, he will tell you what needs to be done to make it better. He may give you medicine for your rabbit.

My pet's fact sheet

Try making a fact sheet about your pet rabbit. Copy the headings on this page, or you can make up your own! Then write in the correct information about your rabbit.

Brown back
White stripe
Long brown ears
Fluffy tail
Twitching nose

Leave a space to stick in a photograph or draw a picture of your rabbit. Then label all of your pet's special features.

Name: Floppy

Birthday: September 28

Weight: 4½ pounds (2 kilograms)

Favorite fresh food: Carrot

Best game: Hiding in a pipe

Veterinarian's name: Mark Evans

Veterinary assistant's name: Thaddeus Weir

Vet's office telephone number: 555-1234

Injections
Your rabbit can pick up germs from wild animals when it is outside. To make sure it does not get ill, take it to your vet to have inoculations every six months.

Index